This or That Pets

Is a FERRET or a RAT the Pet for Me?

by Cara Krenn

PEBBLE
a capstone imprint

Published by Pebble, an imprint of Capstone
1710 Roe Crest Drive, North Mankato, Minnesota 56003
capstonepub.com

Copyright © 2025 by Capstone. All rights reserved. No part of this publication may be reproduced in whole or in part, or stored in a retrieval system, or transmitted in any form or by any means, electronic, mechanical, photocopying, recording, or otherwise, without written permission of the publisher.

Library of Congress Cataloging-in-Publication Data is available on the Library of Congress website.
ISBN: 9780756579272 (hardcover)
ISBN: 9780756579227 (paperback)
ISBN: 9780756579234 (ebook PDF)

Summary: Silky coats. Cute faces. Both rats and ferrets are smart, fun pets! Compare these two active pets side by side. Which needs a bigger cage? Which lives longer? Which pet needs more exercise? Learn the answers to these questions and more. Then decide which one might make the best pet for you!

Image Credits
Capstone Studio: Karon Dubke, 6, 9, 11; Getty Images: Douglas Sacha, 13, JuergenBosse, 12, Marcia Fernandes, 16, Osobystist, 10, shironosov, 15; Shutterstock: Bilanol, 4, Eric Isselee, 8, Irina Vasilevskaia, Cover (top), 5, IrinaK, 20, Ksenia Sterkhova, 17, Luvtinytoes, 14, 21, Maliutina Anna, 19, Mary Swift, Cover (bottom), Natasha Pankina, background (throughout), XxongZoo, 7; Superstock: Mary Evans Picture Library/Jean-Michel Labat, 18

Editorial Credits
Editor: Carrie Sheely; Designer: Bobbie Nuytten; Media Researcher: Jo Miller; Production Specialist: Whitney Schaefer

Dedication: For Luke

Any additional websites and resources referenced in this book are not maintained, authorized, or sponsored by Capstone. All product and company names are trademarks™ or registered® trademarks of their respective holders.

Printed and bound in China. PO 5834

Table of Contents

Getting a New Pet 4
Space Needs 8
Cheap or Costly 10
More or Less Activity 12
Smelly or Not 14
Cuddles and Snuggles 16
Short or Long Lives 18
Which Pet Is Best for You? 20
    Glossary 22
    Read More 23
    Internet Sites 23
    Index 24
    About the Author 24

Words in **bold** are in the glossary.

Getting a New Pet

Sniff! Whiskers twitch, and noses smell. Rats and ferrets are smart and friendly. These **curious** pets are ready to play!

Rats and ferrets have some things in common. Both pets are **social**. They can form strong bonds with their owners. But they're also different in some ways.

Which pet is best for you? It depends. Rats are easy to keep. They may be good pets for busy families. Ferrets are very active! They need more attention.

Where do you live? Some places have laws that don't let people have pet ferrets. California and Hawaii do not allow pet ferrets. There may be **local** laws about having pet ferrets too.

Space Needs

Rats and ferrets need large cages. They need room to play. They also need space for food, water, and **bedding**. They need a place to go to the bathroom too.

How big of a cage do you need? It depends on how many rats or ferrets you have. Both pets do best in pairs. Ferrets are larger animals than rats. They need bigger cages.

Cheap or Costly

Some costs for ferrets and rats are alike. Both need yearly visits to a **veterinarian**. It is fairly cheap to feed them. But ferrets tend to cost more.

You can get a ferret from a pet store or adopt one from a rescue shelter. They can cost about $500. Ferrets often need more veterinarian care than rats. Ferrets need shots called **vaccinations**. Rats do not need these.

More or Less Activity

Rats and ferrets need exercise. Rats can run on a wheel in their cage. They also need about one hour of playtime outside their cage daily. Ferrets need about four hours of playtime outside their cage every day. Ferrets can even learn to go on walks.

Rats and ferrets love toys! Rat toys can be simple. They can be toilet paper rolls or cardboard boxes. Many ferrets like hard balls and toys with bells. They often **hoard** toys.

Smelly or Not

Rats **groom** themselves. They do not smell much. Rats are very clean and do not need baths.

Ferrets have a musky smell that some people do not like. Keeping your ferret's cage clean will help with its smell.

Cuddles and Snuggles

Do you want a cuddly pet? Rats are calm and gentle. Most like to be held.

Ferrets can be cuddly too. They may lie with their owners on a blanket. They might even snuggle into a sweatshirt. Always handle ferrets carefully. They can bite when excited or scared.

Short or Long Lives

Getting a pet is a big decision. Both rats and ferrets need good care throughout their lives.

Rats have a short life span of about two to four years. Ferrets live about eight years.

Which Pet Is Best for You?

Both rats and ferrets make great pets. This activity can help you find out which one might be best for you.

What You Need:

- pencil or pen
- paper

What You Do:

1. Draw a picture of a rat. Around your picture, write the things you like most about rats. Use what you learned about rats from this book to help you. Draw a line from each word to your picture.

2. Next, draw a picture of a ferret. Write down what you like most about ferrets. Draw a line from each word to your picture.

3. Count the lines for each pet. Which pet has more? This might be the pet for you!

Glossary

bedding (BED-ing)—materials used to make an animal's bed

curious (KYUR-ee-uhs)—eager to explore and learn

groom (GROOM)—to keep clean

hoard (HORD)—to collect and hide away

local (LO-kuhl)—related to a small area, such as a town or city

social (SOH-shuhl)—wanting to be near people or animals

vaccination (vak-suh-NAY-shun)—a shot that helps keep an animal or person healthy

veterinarian (vet-ur-uh-NER-ee-uhn)—a doctor trained to take care of animals

Read More

Lowe, Lindsey. *Rodents*. Tucson, AZ: Brown Bear Books, 2023.

Polinsky, Paige V. *My Pet Ferret*. Minneapolis: Bellwether, 2020.

Thielges, Alissa. *Curious About Ferrets*. Mankato, MN: Amicus, 2023.

Internet Sites

Easy Science for Kids: Rats and Their Different Types
easyscienceforkids.com/all-about-rats/

Ferret Facts
pethealthpharmacy.com/ferret-facts/

National Geographic Kids: 10 Facts About Rats!
natgeokids.com/nz/discover/animals/general-animals/facts-about-rats/

Index

activity levels, 6

being held, 16, 17

biting, 17

cages, 8, 9, 12, 15

costs, 10, 11

exercise, 12

grooming, 14

laws, 7

life spans, 19

playtime outside cages, 12

smelliness, 14, 15

socialness, 5

toys, 13

vaccinations, 11

About the Author

Cara Krenn writes children's books and for a variety of kids' magazines. The topics she writes about range from trash trucks to magical creatures. Cara loves the beach, dance music, and morning walks with her cowardly dog. She is a graduate of the University of Notre Dame and lives in sunny San Diego, California, with her husband, twin daughters, and son.